D0687070

THE HISTORY
OF THE
GROWTH OF HEAVEN

by Andrei Codrescu

license to carry a gun
a serious morning

ANDREI CODRESCU

THE HISTORY
OF THE GROWTH
OF HEAVEN

A VENTURE BOOK
GEORGE BRAZILLER
NEW YORK

811.5

The Author gratefully acknowledges the following
people and magazines for their involvement with some
of these poems: Tom Veitch, Isthmus, Alternative Press,
Search for Tomorrow, Tractor, Toothpaste, Poetry
(Chicago), nadine, The World, The World Anthology,
Another World, Ironwood, Buffalo Stamps, Gum, Man-
root, Stuffed Crocodile, Bastard Angel, Doones, Defiance,
Deserted Times, Big Sky & Fervent Valley.

Contents

Face Portrait

More

c.|

The History of the Growth of Heaven

Moments of Absolute Truth

THE HISTORY
OF THE
GROWTH OF HEAVEN

FACE PORTRAIT

"*What will his crimes become, now that her hands have gone to sleep?*"

Us

Oh I believe that all of us real poets string pickers
all of you great geniuses of my changing crystals
all of you and all beasts
have been growing hungry from a fast in us.
Now now here is the presence of mind
needed to stand up in the refrigerator and turn on the light
spouting from the butter, eerie eggs
of mind presence snowing near the gardens.
Dear God, Cauliflower & Broccoli are so Beautiful Together!
And the frozen ducks in the cracked cellophane pushing
a slice of pizza into the side of a clam can!
And the cheese singing!
Oh I believe that all of us
are ready!

Face Portrait

I am a man of face like another is "a man
of position" or "a man of hair." I take
things at their face values and the weight
of this world slides off
my face like a skier over snow. I live
through my face like others "get through
the day." It is not a particularly handsome
face, rather a gross sensual
barrage meant to take the breath out of you.
I imagine death as an epiphany of my face
in which a glow of dying roses clutched
in a diffusion of angles by discarnate hands
descends upon my eyes
and breaks them loose.
While the garters of divine ladies
snap and escape with my ears.
Still, I am alive and in this season of my face
there is the joy of sinning without surgery!

work

at night the day is constantly woken up
by exploding dream objects
until all our days are tired
and collapse on our hearts like loud
zippers breaking in the middle.
i sleep in the daytime with my head on the piano.
i sleep at night too standing on the roof.
i sleep all the sleep that is given me plus
the sleep of those who can't sleep and the sleep
of great animals who lie wounded
and unable to sleep.
i'm dead tired from the work everyone does
ceaselessly around me, from the work the morning
crowds are going to do after they are thrown up
by the thousand mouths of toast and cologne
into the buses and subways,
from the work the plants do to get water
from the labors of beasts looking for meat
from the labors of speaking replying writing
from the work going on inside me with a million
greedy cells beating the shit out of each other
from the work of the sun turning around
and the earth turning around it.
i'm tired in general and sleepy in particular.
i have a great desire to move elsewhere.

New York

The streets of this strange metropolis . . .
Frozen spaghetti, fear of ghosts . . .
The scarred pavements
have a very eloquent texture
of bums woven with empty bottles and soot,
an ancient tapestry.
On this curious mattress one bounces looking for sex.
Layers and layers of sex
for each layer of you. . . Tongue overlaps
with ten thousand other tongues,
genitals are enmeshed in so many other genitals
that a ball of flame floats permanently around the city.
If you think this is rough
you don't know the heart of it because it's
silky and funny and feels
like the breeze of hereafter

tête-à-tête

my body, spill-proof but not quite,
is full of grinning groceries, my liver
dreams of paté. my heart
makes the soup red. my head
stuffs itself with birds. even
my fingernails look good in jello.
the trick is to bring in each
dish at the right time in the dim
candlelight. the trick
is to surprise your guest with the ease
with which you delve into
yourself

trains

trains run on emotion not
good advice. the southern pacific
runs on a wet appetite. the trans-
siberian is loaded with boxes filled
with the tears of russians
going to hell. romanian rail-
roads run only in the rain and not
every time. on french
trains women give birth. and the rails
themselves are licked shiny every-
day by the tongues of museum
curators

a grammar

i was dead and i wanted peace
then i was peaceful and not quite dead yet
then i was in my clothes
and i took them off and then
there was too much light
and night fell
then i wanted to talk to somebody
and i spoke ecstatically
and i was answered on time in every language
in a beautiful way
but i felt unloved and everyone
came to love me

still there is something running
and i can't catch it
i am always behind

The Army asks for your son
the Sea asks for your daughter
and you yourself find it hard to live in a world of so many
                    beautiful women
who all want you

the best side of me

tomatoes squashes and cauliflowers intrigue me immensely
with their lewd proposals
and their making the stability of my appetite burst
with the lust of their red yellow and white chewiness.
you're chewy, i'm looney.
i dream of soft furry things with inward claws
lodged in my brain
who open when it rains.
then whole cities built around a globe of waving squash.
we float backwards into early tickles of consciousness.
faces pull through complicated threads of greasy smiles.
my friend peter chewing on his model airplane.
the stretched frown of my tomato nanny.
if i ever walk out of this dream
my work is all over. my body releases
the captives from ten thousand labors.

what want ye

i'm a fish a strange fish not to myself tho
bathing in the cave-like
aspect of the world
without clothes   the kind of fish
you have for dessert after a main course of raw meat
or a look at politics   a la king
to myself tho i'm the kind of fish you have for breakfast
while the sun bathes the room in its best   the room's best
ah to be the kind of fish in the *sun's* best
ah i want that

the great poets are not in the language but in business
because what poet can make cut production costs equal
infinite compassion, offhand, in a matter of fact way
and in a tone that excludes misunderstanding? not only
do the great poets now sit outside language manipulating
the heart but also the great readers of poetry who,
stunned in the past by the printed page, are now free
to have dinner and board a bus in the company of sheer
poetry with not a thought for their own failings which,
quite apart from their bodies, they now take to the
doctors to get fixed? in our time, we elevate details
to the power of numbers, to the place where concrete
representation has flown the coop, and one day we will
see ourselves translated in machinery and this, thank
god, will be the day when i will unscrew my head with
the silence of my surroundings and go to sleep forever.

sea sickness

dancers strapped to canoes is
what the morning brings. they are tied
to a perpetual dance.
hooded folks in lighthouses
count on their fingers as the day
gets brighter. everywhere
dancing is either law
or crime. i have no particular
taste for this world. i am looking
for an utterly still completely
dead hotel.

MORE

Early Fix

It's been like this every morning:
a click and the pattern
is irretrievably set
by an authoritarian hand pressed
palm down on your forehead.
All day you walk with the map
of someone's life shining from under
the roots of your hair.
Since everyone (as if you cared)
assumes now that your head
is a hand
you go on pouring coffee through the lights
of your brain.
Every thought is a missing ship.
The little babies in the pictures turn
into voracious gypsies
reading your script

Opium for Britt Wilkie

The beautiful swimmer the extremely shy
opium eater touches his hat
in homage to the great pool lying
still at the feet of the crow. The
snow on his hat says
something to me but I am a weapon
with a small vocabulary
hanging from a deer horn rack. And
then he plunges into the blue water into
our afternoon. Oh hello there. We are
squeezing a string of smoke to cause our melo-
dramatic hearts to ripple up and down
the spine of the world. But he just
swims on sending a slight metallic shock
through us. OK. When we will meet
again he will be swimming back having
brought a big wet clock with him from the other
side of this home

Manifesto

It's opium we need not truth.
Unless we are and we are morally pinned to the wall
with a gold stake. I am
pinned to your forehead, Karl Marx, like a
butterfly to a skirt.
The one way out is through blood, your
blood. Here, surrounded by the serenity
and transparence of opium
we sail toward the island of your blood.
When we stop we experience night.
As we go on the light of day bathes us.

Alberta

When Alberta swims the whole night in the creek behind
the house where I sit counting the rooms, I want to
send owls in the branches above her with the results
of my count. 13 rooms, Alberta, 13 rooms! Or maybe
a thousand! But what owls, indeed what beasts, can last
the impact of her smooth, wet body leaving a trail of
warm dark men in the phosphorescent water . . . Two fishes
mate in the depression between her breasts! Waiting
their turn, all the other creatures in the creek are
emanating a light that messes up my count. How many
rooms did I say? Then she speaks from my faucet when
I drink and the glass of water in my hand shimmers with
an invisible lust. At the end of all these rooms, at
the end, indeed, of all rooms, there is Alberta swimming
on and her strokes inside my bloodcells culminate in
light, in small blue explosions.

sit down

when i sit in my chair i am a link in an atomic
party playing "telephone" by whispering the original word
into smaller and smaller ears
in the (always unexpressed) hope that the end of the line
is soon reached and The End will
stand up and shout out loud what i've been hearing all along
the word that's been driving me crazy up the wall
into the frying pan of the world!
the cumquats embedded in the land
shriek as they are spanked into the edges
of the white plate!
allowing for the thousand distortions
that make us laugh, tell me,
has anyone ever said anything?
my mind is filled with snowflakes of soft things.

good morning

sometimes when they shut off the faucets
i think of chinese mailmen
how they must feel holding
birds full of letters.
i would like to walk with them
into the small
circumcisions at the top of houses
through which hands protrude waiting
for telegrams.
because this is a country of telegrams
we emerge from holding shocked doorknobs
between our knees

Opium for Archie Anderson

I am home eating a heart A very slow
heart! A languishing pregnancy
pushes its lazy baby through the tenth
year! We hear the news under-
water Morsel after morsel
of hysteria Look I am home with the
bride She is lying
on a bed of artichokes with her heart hovering
over her overripe belly And
she hasn't been speaking for years except
to me! And
I lie! I lie a lot! I will
eat this heart I will go out and tell Look
I ate a heart I will
do it again! I will
eat your heart if only you could
be seized with such miracles! If only
you could rot so graciously on a bed
of artichokes If only you could
drive me south! Drive me deaf! If
you could bubble like mineral waters! If you
could walk up my ladders! Human
ladders!

Crossed Hands

One day our noses will be in heaven
while our arms will roast in hell, the body
is a watch composed of moralities with different
places of encampment. Take then
this body home with you and love it in general
like you love your grandmother.
She has long since been entered in a log
of love stains on a sheet of dark
and with her image we will knot
frantic new bones.
All resurrection must begin right away.

The Order of a Spring Day

It's all in order that you may
wake up beating your Coca Cola against
the paint on the wall
while the birches outside are beating
up your girlfriend.
March tunes on the window.
It's all in order that you may
harmonize with the sky inside your dilated
pupils blinking at the clouds
and at the pain of her wild
tits banging on the copper bowl outside the door.
It's all so that you may suddenly wake up
on the other side of the needle.
It's all in the order of the day.

Architecture

"Why not call it Egypt?" (*Dick Gallup*)

Your pubic hair is the apex of a lovely
triangle rising through each day of my life
to complete a pyramid being secretly built
in my blood.
The mythical import of this construct
is then placed in the perspective of what the dead
are building under the streams, in what
imitations of us are being plotted by governments
in the cheaper materials, in rawhide
and in silver telephones

visitación! visitación!
i had both my hands on the red telephone!
maría! maría! mother of god!
the cracks in the ceiling are lines in the palm!
my fingers are sweating with blessings!
the honey of the apocalypse is upon your soft body!
maría of the motelroom ceiling!
stars of the red telephone!

Junkie Heaven

It's a sort of cemetery except
only hearts are buried here.
The rest is taken by train and burnt.
When the grass is tall enough
sheep are brought in and left to graze
until their wool turns red.
Then the season turns bad and everyone leaves
little transistor radios on the graves.

rain blows my eyelashes upwards toward
the spot of light which is my face
which is being circled by a dove.
i am lying under a piano
and your beautiful white feet are on my naked belly.
the rain of the Lord is in my heart.

your fantastic outlines

your fantastic outlines, inlines, mines and hollows
drop through my aroused pools
like heat sinking through the thermometer
of charlie manson's heart. revelation
of the love of being here.
this book of love will be written
out of the sheer propelling of my body into
those parts of you where foreign people drive
heavy trucks into the night of the best
love poems ever. but new. but best. but free
of mild chances, of robberies of love. free
of you even
as we float upstream
slipping
into the core of another element

THE HISTORY
OF THE
GROWTH OF HEAVEN

"*tout ce qui existe est situé*" said max jacob and
one day my situation was such that only a detached, religious
and ecstatic perspective could bring home all that i was.
since i was nothing in particular at that time i became a
monk because it seemed to me that monks had no ego, only
visions and a sense of humor. i am still a monk to the
extent that this is true. my professional services when
i am in robes consist of techniques for sabotaging
history with the aid of god. so to speak.

To the Virgin as She Now Stands
to the Monk after a Beatles Movie

This is no cell, Holy Woman,
this is a lookout into the shape of that boundless forgery,
into the outline of the Devil's face
when the smog opens up to let us view
the rugged cliffs of his face.
This, of course, is a Monk's crossview
of the book between the legs of naked ladies,
those splinters of you
who go to the movies by themselves
to make love in the dark.
For a flash the singer reaches out on the wire
of your Presence, through the screen,
it hurts to see the waste.
Paralysis of upper vastness, Virgin,
caste out, caste in
of my race.
The terror of your cunt is the beauty of your face.

Faith Relearned

A letter to Father Veitch

Faith is the evidence of things I've wasted,
the evidence of things not seen
maybe the canals of Amsterdam could tell you
where I've been all these years:
partly behind my shoulder blades
scratching the skin's illusion of secret showers,
partly fighting an ancient war,
partly trying to fit a rug on this floor,
Woolworth's, $9.95, no good,
and partly monking in my cell:
the cheese they feed you here muffles your yell,
its holes let in the others',
its holes look out of you:
the things they've seen inside my night
draw blood from the hinges of lovers,
from the owls of Holland at night.
What I see through my cheese holes is
that view the crucifix has
from inside the iron shirt of the Knight
as he bops past crazy windmills

My Next Book

My next book will have a poem for each
Saint dropped by the Church,
33 poems in all,
the longest one for Saint George
who was the longest man in the world when added
to the end of his lance.
I will put a little cross by each poem
meaning "here lies,"
a very deceptive move since no one
will lie in there,
no one, not even the Monk
who will be out thinking of girls
what are poems?

The Sin of Wanting a New Refrigerator

Sin is impervious
to past transmutations
yet this is how it happened:
I desired
the bareness of my cell to open
in the vaster bareness of a new refrigerator,
it,
the refrigerator,
having come all the way from the First Avenue of my
New York days,
from the fruit stand of the dark
fat merchant. He opened it up
in another Universe: the milk bottles inside
lit up like Angels. First Avenue
refrigerated. I was a penny short
and I still am.
They tell me here that new refrigerators
are forbidden, oh
that penny had in it a sin
as elemental as the copper
it was made of

More about Poems

I want to write down the life
that could be my life if I insisted
if I pulled up a corner of the cloth to let the lady
with the groceries
have a look at my cock,
flash of storks running errands for God.
I want to perfect a partial view
through a hole in my cloth,
a slanted recording, a window hangup,
not mindful of the undistorted door,
of the remarkable way.
I ought to repair my life with the grease of Poems:
the bourgeois at war with the monk.
Oh, the volume of the devil's lease!

The Indecent Assumptions,
The Slaughter Songs

For Ignatio de Loyola

This is vengeance.
Everything that moves is vengeance or else
is a lost face. A lost bet,
a Tibet for the aged, for the slippery
rock foot.
At eighty, the age of youth for most trees,
I will begin the writing of my soul,
of the way it was set in place by a hand more precise
than a lover's.
Oh, inaccurate lovers Oh, washing machines!
The upside down face
of the turn of the century.
The turn of horseshit into bullshit.
Vengeance. Your dish, Ignatio,
seasoned with fried simpletons,
with Knights of the Book.
They thought you would hand it to them.
Oh, God, their Bible, oh, Azvoth, their Kalevala,
Odin, their Mein Kampf,   (Their: Mein)
Oh, Buddha of the Mountain, their little Red Book,
little, no matter how little,
but give it to them.
Maybe my avenging head pulling at the end of the hook
will resume its inventions,
will open up as their Book
of the indecent assumptions,
of the slaughter songs

The Status of the Monk

is not moveable
though your block might be getting worse
and the crickets are moving out. From porch to porch
the twisted ladies have
turned their knitting needles on themselves,
housewife collage.
A people's militia to meet the needs of love.
But I have nothing left to hate.
I remain medieval
no matter what you do to me,
perched on myself like an endless tapestry.
God put his suitcase down to rest on it.
The women try to guess its contents.

About Photography

I hate photographs,
those square paper Judases of the world,
the fakers of love's image of all things.
They show you parents where the frogs of doom
are standing under the heavenly flour,
they picture grassy slopes
where the bugs of accident whirr twisted
in the flaws of the world.
It is weird,
this violence of particulars
against the unity of being

For the Dancer in my Head

Only the dead is cold like the dead in its ice cube.
I hope the dancer in my head leaves me alone tonight,
alone, and lean.
Bishop Henley dreamt of an ice palace
he was about to melt with his burning faith
one cold Christmas, 19. . .
He knew of a living woman, a warmth lender.
She's trapped inside the dancer in my head,
her words are thick like her thighs
when she speaks.
Et nos servasti eternali sanguine fusso.
That is a reference to blood
that had the priests of old spill the communion

Attempt to Spell, Incantate and Annoy

May his eyes go on unblinking
and his ears from bells unhurting
may he go the way of wires . . .
I can't write spells, I'm a monk.
One is constantly expected to write about his environment,
the melting stuff, the mood of his sins,
the geology of the billionth of a second,
I am even supposed to confess my environment
to an asthma struck intermediary of a not-so-instantaneous God,
do you, Holy Ones, suppose
that we are made of thick flesh, rawhide, penicillin,
or is the Confessor really Nylon Man
when he chooses to rip open his ecclesiastic cloth
and go chasing after bank robbers?
I had to put this heresy down on paper
this poem is a heretic environment
how do you confess it?

The First Icon with Gun

Flemish style, late 17th century:
the Virgin holds a gun
not the baby.
Artist, unknown.

Danger

For M. G. Stephens

The dangerous point
in the development of a monk is not
the sudden unveiling of a pair of fat thighs
under the horsehair blanket at night,
or the sight of an asshole in the shower,
bending for soap,
the real danger is the magic he can perform
after he gets his head together
in regard to the world.
The Wizard that rides on the whipped senses

Junk Mail

Junk mail. A gun for a dollar.
This one dollar deal has changed the face
of all I thought was mine,
and it still cries from the enormous pain
of being screwed inside my shoes,
made to reside upright,
both eyes directed into the heart of "Daily News"
and snow will be here soon.
The stamp stares me down with "Man on the Moon."
I smell the blades of cold
traveling this side of mail without zip code,
glued to the wide phantoms of cars going out
of style. My snowed in prayers will relieve my heart
of bombs and rifles.
For a while

Stupor at the End of May

What some mistake for me meditating
is a giant stupor with a black hood
sitting crossed legged at the end of May, counting
the days till Christmas.
Stupor, flat and simple, the overture
to the large thoughts of the Rectory cow
underfed but happy in her
buzzard shadow

From A.C. to A.C.

Maria
is simply Maia
with the solar R
in her womb

Sarrasin's Wealth Song

boo hoo hoo and boo ha ha
seeing him shit you'd think that he's ready
to enter the heavens holding a cow
by her teats.
this is my cow. and see this, god:
i'm busy; the welfare of chickens,
mushed corn for the rabbits, grease
for the ax and check the balls
of my horses.
i'm a bread maker besides.
so am i. let him go,
he's a busy man.
boo hoo hoo and boo ha ha

The Spirit of Romance

lit the candles.
In the exact middle of the Father's Prayer
it switched rhythm and recited itself upside down.
The whole thing recited upside down
invokes the devil.
The two halves of the prayer
as they stood back to back, ready for a duel,
gave me a mysterious feeling,
the candles posed for breath
like birth, the Spirit
of Romance

Howdy

Before I was a monk I had a cat.
She was darker than Buddha, the great, the elementary.
Actually she was black
and she liked bad wine which she licked
from my glass when I went out
looking for girls.
Her drunk look was of drowned dogs,
of sorrowful junk,
she had seen my brother François
hung from his laces outside his Lady's castle.
From the height of her whiskers it looked like the facts of heaven.
Now I'm a monk and Howdy,
t'was her name,
peeps backward into my mouth from a ceiling
of frosted eternity.
The bad wine links us like a birthday feeling

Charlie Manson and the Weather of Heavens

The barometer. The weather of the higher
regions. What gods blow by?
Did you feel the gloating of Pan who is
or isn't sad today?
On your naked shoulders? (so naked
that one is shocked in front of them
like against a drop of dew under the microscope,
so raw, so intricate, so silvery!)
The cold days up there
gather a crop of warriors down here
where Charlie Manson tries to prevent it
heroically, perhaps
too slowly.
As for me I'm slow by nature, by shell,
by crazy spells of winter thaws.
Charlie aspires to my calm
while I envy the revolving of his claws

The Boone Family

an autohagiography

First came Peter Boone,
a unique madman whose inventions are at the root
of my invention of him.
Born in Istanbul and dead in Vietnam.
Then the "dead" bothered me and he didn't die in Vietnam.
He entered a monk
and his first name became Calvin.
Exit Saturn from the 2nd House of his Chart.
The light of his name
revealed him some place in his heart.
The power of which tears me apart.

MOMENTS OF ABSOLUTE TRUTH

"When the gods die
the myths
are lifted off our backs.
Peace be with them.
They were heavy."

TOM CLARK

the good spirit

the spirit of this room is dead. it was a very good spirit.
it kept the tea warm and it put me to sleep
it fastened our love and it took good care of the heart.
it shone over the lower east side.
1 A.M: things are unveiled, we are unprotected at night
and i want to plant an insane bomb in my own liver.
so i will never meet my edges again.
if only this disgust would leave me alone.

history

in 1946 there was my mother inside whom
i was still hiding.
in 1953 i was small enough to curl behind a tire
while the man with the knife passed.
in 1953 also i felt comfortable under the table
while everyone cried because stalin was dead.
in 1965 i hid inside my head
and the colors were formidable.
and just now at the end of 1971
i could have hidden inside a comfy hollow in the phone
but i couldn't find the entrance

breakfast elegy

ever since the abandonment of courtship
i haven't had a good time in the world   a city
is a bomb in your liver which lets *you*
set the timer   when the sun is out
you don't want to blow up   love love
i am responsible for the welfare of the idiot masses
i carry the darkness of ages on my back
i carry a knife in my boot   a purple water issues
from our genetic taps   what can i say
that does not instantly jell as the sugar in birds
crystallizes in flight

true late

it is late at night and i am writing true poems
because there is nothing to prey on!
i will tell you now, for ex, that i am a jew,
something that in the daytime
i won't even whisper. i will
tell you everything you want to know
because it doesn't feel either like july
or like december. my heart is heavy,
happy heavy like a foreign city at night
in the rain in september. i have just come
from seeing ted berrigan shoot up
and it made me sad. the sadness that is
traveling through the world at this hour
is giving us its best wishes!
i would like to stand up and be a big piss.
but there is always the "ashes of your hand"
massaging my heart

why write

i've always looked for joy as a pretext to write
but could not or would not
fall face down upon that knot of pain which seems
to make even the simplest things
a complete and frightening mystery.
this way i have avoided being torn
by the terrific closeness with that heart-shaped weapon
which makes us die. i have left out
important fragments of my life. i've taken only
the juice out of the squalor. i have avoided
loving more than i *could* love.

eugenio montale in california

and here where a new life
sprouts into a mild
anxiety from the orient
your words, like the scales on a dying fish,
flash into sunset

watching ted shoot up
is both sad and mythical. it makes me feel
like an ant staring at a vast body of water.

an inexplicable sadness for home!

f e a r

fear is my way
of not being here although
i am afraid of falling asleep for fear
of a frightening thing taking place in my absence.
i am also
afraid of the axe i keep behind the bed hoping
that no one will come in or rather
that someone will
and there will be blood.
sitting there in the dark seeing myself kill
over and over
is not fear,
it is pleasure
though when the awareness of pleasure floats up
and i learn that it is pleasure
i become very afraid.
this new house is fear
of the unknown neighbors stretching for miles
in each direction with only
space for houses with no one in them
space for dark windows over basements filled with fear.
the long stone walk from the door
to the top of the stairs
has three major checkpoints of fear:
the cottage on the right where the spooks sit
on the bicycle chains,
the old jew's apartment with the curtains drawn

over the candle light
and finally the stairs themselves going up
through minor and major stations of fear
which at the age of six are like the days themselves,
long, inexorable.
and now the fear of even writing about fear
the fear of awareness

A Point

This then is the point in my life
(a point not in me or in the middle)
where a light flashes down from the mountain
with a chinese determination
to have my body yield a series
of moral statements.
To say what it feels like to lie.
Or to judge the import of a slashed throat
under the dirty shirt collar.
Or to determine how agreeable the death
of one's mother is
in the dimming business hours.
Later this point becomes me as I
reappear in town peddling a substance
taken from the bodies of flagellant monks

books

death covers me with fine dust.
i love used fat books. they are
like used fat bodies coming out of sleep
covered with fingerprints and shiny
snail trails.
i wish to read the way i love:
jumping from mirror to mirror like a drop of oil
farther and farther from my death.
but god gives us fat books and fat bodies
to use for different reasons
and less a metaphor i cannot say
what haunts me

star book

there are many books about the zodiac
that mirrors us. from each
page shines the lion of a yet
unlived day. the best
book is the stars themselves right
before dawn when the chill of your mind
sucks itself home. the summer
of california is the best
binding!

what am i talking about when i'm talking
things look real
they freak me out

poem

the supreme test of one's poem
is in the bathtub standing up naked hands
above the head like a gothic christ
and if the picture in the mirror is of a fat
belly swaying between the forks of a black grin
it's still OK! but no poem

Alice's Brilliance

Her brilliance consists in colors. She can sink her teeth
into a nuance from one thousand steps like the Lone Ranger.
She sees rainbows, desert sunsets and Dutch Boy factories
in every drop of water and in this tablecloth. There is
nothing doesn't come to her for therapy because she can,
you see, cure grey desperate people by yanking the veil
from their eyes and revealing the brilliant dazzle even
in the patches of their pants. Everyone is richer for her
presence. Since she came to town we move more graciously,
there is coquetry in the air, the trees bow gallantly. *I
don't want to upset my colors over you, buster,* says the
traffic cop handing out a rolled papyrus with a ticket
written on it in gold ink and gothic characters. His
pearl-handled revolver sways gently on his curved hip.
The old truckdrivers even exude an air of civilization,
a thin blanket of pink. All the rougher colors gather
by the river and tell violet stories shifting their eyes
like needles in the ochre light. At times her brilliance
attains peaks of perfection and we feel pierced by unknown and unnamed colors that then stay perched like
vultures on our hearts and defend us against death.

talismanic ceremony for lucian,
march 9, 1971, intersection church, san francisco

since he's not jewish
and he won't get circumcised
or bar mitzvahd

since he's not christian
and he won't get christened
or given first communion

since he's not a baby anymore
and too big to wear
pink and blue pajamas

i now pronounce him a kid

this is a solemn ceremony
in which
his mommy
is giving him back
his umbilical cord

to protect him from this world
with a talisman
from another

this is then a solemn ceremony
in which
his father
is giving him a new name

LUCIAN CODRESCU

to make him the first

San Francisco for Whomever

"Whomever," this is for you!
The streets of this beautiful town
bend minds all day long.
They bend them up the hills and then they blow them
down the sparrow sights.
When you open your eyes something else
opens hers.
Cubic miles of raw cotton in pink laundry bags to
swim into.
At the end of a tickle of blue you loaf away.
Your hips pass you by
oh pictures of my life in every window
with faces of new girlfriends
in blue sails flying the turtles
from these red eggs.
There is a storm in your walking motors
and there is the beginning of the world lying ahead

late night, san francisco

so few things to write about
when there is a sky full of the electrical lights of san francisco

stilling the lights in your head from the left
and the sea some two feet away filling the other ear
with the sounds of all the things you ever wanted to say.
the wind the horse thief takes whatever is left over
from that music i cherish inside winelike in the airtight heart.

there is nothing here now.
the whining after the unplugging of the world.

Thieves, Seasons

At the end of summer they burn the house we live in.
See the hooks of a change
bigger than words
clawing at the shut veins in the leaves.
When the thieves come to scavenge
I put your hand over my mouth
not really a mouth.
Only a bowl of fermenting yuca
in the half coconut shell.
Dear Mom,
they've stolen my mouth from under her hand.
Now they can burn
everything. The winter seagulls are already
at the guts of alien carrion. I don't
recognize a thing.
Supreme thieves are in the order of greater events:
they leave a mythical confusion on which we build
our next lives

new morning

relieved of phantoms   light   with a new shirt on!
i take on a new name   a new totemic animal
i'm not looking for what i used to look for   i found it!
my person, the gist of which is violence,
gives me back my art, the gist of which is *staying loose*!
the programmatic, the unessential is a shadow
without body moving by echo-location out of the world!
my eyes are a heart   late afternoon sun
i bit my finger as hard as i could to make myself cry
i could only smile